The Soccer Nutrition Guide

Mirsad Hasic

Copyright © Mirsad Hasic
All rights reserved.
ISBN: 1494302543
ISBN-13: 978-1494302542

DEDICATION

I dedicate this book to my wife.

CONTENTS

Introduction 1
The Macronutrients 5
   Carbohydrates 6
   Protein 12
   Fat 16
The Micronutrients 22
   Vitamins and Soccer 23
   Minerals 30
Diets 39
   The Atkins Diet? 39
   Organic Diet 41
   Soccer Diet Example 44
Fluid 46
   Hydration 46
   Dehydration 48
   Water 49
   Sports Drinks 53
   Alternative Hydration 58
Game Food 61
   The morning game 61
   Evening game 63
   Post-Game 64
Myths, Tips and Maximum Performance 65
   Common myths 66
   Maximize your performance levels 69
   Nutrition checklist 74
Ending… 76

ACKNOWLEDGMENTS

I would like to thank my family for their support.

Introduction

Nutrition will either make or break your soccer game depending on whether you get enough of it or too little.

Unfortunately, not so many amateur players are too aware of the importance of proper nutrition and the role it has in successful soccer.

Ever heard the statement, "we are what we eat? Well it's true, it really is. Every cell in our body functions or malfunctions based on what we feed on.

I like to think about nutrition and soccer in terms of the following metaphor: Imagine you're a car, any car you want, and your food is what the car uses for its fuel.

Well, if you don't fill the tank up when it's getting empty, then you're not going to get very far.

And if you fill the tank with substandard fuel, then it's not going to run anywhere near as well as it would do on premium fuel.

This all makes perfect logical sense, right?

OK, now take your body back and become you again.

Food is still the fuel that runs your engine, but just like in the case with the car, if you don't have enough of it then you're not going to get very far.

Furthermore, if you consume substandard food, as in junk meals and processed snacks, then you can't possibly expect to perform at you optimal level.

This is because the food you're using for fuel is not providing you with the nutritional value required to function at your best.

It's not enough to just eat; you also need to eat the right things.

If your car is built for gasoline then it will not run if filled with diesel.

In other words, use the wrong fuel or low quality fuel, and you're on a hiding to nothing.

There was a time when I didn't care too much about what I ate, not even before games and practice sessions.

My preferred pre-game food was a McDonald's meal, usually three cheese burgers, French fries, and a large gassy Coke.

As soon as I began to warm up after these kinds of meals I would feel as though my body was lacking in energy, although I never quite made the connection back in those early days.

I didn't change this behavior until one day when I stumbled upon a short book at the local library. It was entitled 'Soccer Nutrition' or something like that.

I wasn't looking for a book on the topic; I just came across it when searching for something else.

Anyway, I decided to flick through a few of the pages out of curiosity. After just a few minutes of reading, I suddenly felt like a complete idiot.

I came to realize, right there, in the book's introduction pages, that I had wasted so many games, and why?

Because I hadn't been consuming the right kinds of foods, that's why, not even close. Right there and then I understood why I never seemed to have the oomph needed to perform how I always wanted to perform.

That book was to completely change my attitude towards nutrition, forever. It made me realize that soccer was so much more than just being good with the ball.

I borrowed that book and decided to read it cover to cover back at home. Soon afterward I started to follow the advice given in each of the chapters.

I must have written down like a zillion notes as I read through the pages. Despite the dull title, this book actually made a fascinating read.

During the first game, after I had started on my new nutritional regime, my coach took me to one side at the end and asked if I was okay.

He was concerned because he had never seen me play with so much energy before, not ever. I laughed, and just told him that I had decided to take better control of my diet by replacing junk meals with more nutritional foods.

"Don't worry coach," I said, "The only thing I'm on is a good healthy eating plan."

It wasn't only the coach who had noticed this sudden change in my energy and enthusiasm. My teammates were also curious to know my secret.

When I explained that my change had come about simply by eating 'real' food, along with a few other important things (all of which are included in this book), I then inadvertently became the team's one and only expert on all things related to nutrition.

This suited me fine because it kept me alert to the importance of proper eating, and anyway, the best way to learn something is to teach it, so I really was becoming an expert.

After my suggested diet makeover for the team as a whole, almost all of the guys started to play a much better game soon after they had adjusted their eating habits.

That season we ended up finishing in second place. That wasn't bad at all considering our position before the nutritional revolution was second from bottom.

Follow the tips and suggestions as they are outlined in this book, and I can assure you that you'll be able to improve your performance by several levels, not only physically, but improvements to your mental game too.

Eating well really does change the way you feel and function for the better.

A word or warning: Don't cheat!

This is not an area where you can skimp or cut corners, not if you want to reap the full benefits of good nutrition.

Be honest with yourself, be good to your body, and your body will be good to you.

The Macronutrients

You have probably come across the term 'macronutrients' plenty of times in the past, but you might only have a vague idea of what it actually means, as most laypeople do.

In brief, macronutrients are needed to aid growth, metabolism, and many other important bodily functions.

We couldn't survive without them.

There are three types of macronutrient:
1. Carbohydrates
2. Fats (lipids)
3. Proteins

Each of these three types of macronutrients provide the body with energy in varying degrees:
- Fat contains about nine calories of energy per gram.
- Protein contains about four calories per gram.
- Carbohydrate also contains about four calories per gram.

The following is an example of how you can use the above information to interpret the energy content of your food:

Before you take your next snack or meal, take a look at the nutritional 'facts table' on the packet of the product or products that you plan to consume.

Let's say your food item reads 20 grams of carbohydrate, 10 grams of protein, and 25 grams of fat per portion.

As you now know the energy content per gram for each of these macronutrients, you can see that a portion contains 345 calories in total:

Carbs: 20 x 4 + Protein: 10 x 4 + Fat: 25 x 9 Total = *345 calories.*

Carbohydrates

The fuel provided by carbohydrates is the most efficient for the production of energy.

Carbohydrates are stored as glycogen in muscle tissue and in the liver.

Most carbohydrates produce 'slow release' energy. This is because your body does not consume them right away.

In order to feel fit and ready to perform on the field, it is important that soccer players consume a decent quantity of good carbs prior to a game or practice session.

When you are physically active, your muscles will get most of the energy they need from stored glycogen.

It is therefore vital that your body has appropriate levels of glycogen for the muscles to use when they most need it.

With insufficient amounts of glycogen, your body will soon start to tire, and your mental focus and coordination will also suffer as a consequence.

As a soccer player, about 60% of your diet should come from carbohydrates.

Your diet should consist of small, yet regularly-eaten, carb-rich meals.

However, you must remember when planning your diet that not all carbohydrates are good.

There are various forms of carbohydrates out there in the high street stores and you need to know what is what.

The rate at which your body breaks these carbs down and transforms them into glycogen differs greatly from one to the other.

This is why you need to know your carbs. Fortunately, this is not a difficult exercise.

The breakdown-rate of carbohydrates can be measured by using the glycemic index (or GI).

Foods which feature high on the glycemic index are broken down very quickly by the body, whereas foods lower on the scale are broken down much slower.

Eating the wrong type of carbohydrates at the wrong time of day will affect your performance on the field.

You must carefully plan your carbohydrate intake to make sure you obtain and maintain peak energy levels.

For instance, if you are playing a game in the late-afternoon, you should really try to eat a large, single-helping of 'slow' carbohydrates four or five hours before kick-off.

On the other hand, if your game is scheduled for the morning, then you should stock up your energy reserves by eating a small amount of higher GI carbohydrates.

Just remember that having an adequate amount of stored glycogen is vital for your performance during a game.

Playing soccer involves a lot of running around and other high-energy movements, all of which can quickly deplete the body's glycogen levels.

Players who are nicely stocked-up with glycogen will have a great advantage over any of their opponents who are not.

Having enough glycogen means you will be able to run faster, tackle harder, and endure longer.

So in order to maintain your glycogen at an appropriate level you need to consume the right kinds of carbohydrates at the right times, and also make sure you stay hydrated by drinking plenty of fluids at regular intervals.

This is your recipe for success.

So what kind of carbohydrates should you be eating, and when exactly?

Well, one popular choice among soccer players here in my native Sweden, and a personal favorite of mine, is pasta (carbohydrate) and meat sauce (protein/carb) taken 4-5 hours before a game.

This type of meal can be supplemented with bread, potatoes, and rice, followed by a serving of fruit (bananas are an excellent, carb-rich choice).

These types of carbohydrate feature about midway on the glycemic index, which is why they are best consumed a few hours before a game.

If your game starts earlier in the day, then you ought to consume some higher GI carbs.

I like to have muesli, milk, and raisins in this situation, as these foods provide the quick energy boost I need for an early kickoff.

You will need to calculate the appropriate mix of slow and fast carbs for your diet.

Don't worry, this is nowhere near as fiddly, or as time consuming, as it might sound.

In fact, once you get familiar with it all you'll be knocking your regular meals up without giving a second thought to the process.

In the beginning though, you will need to consult a GI table, just until you become familiar with which foods come under what category.

Carbohydrates are absolutely crucial for maintaining a proper soccer diet.

Without the appropriate amount, or types, your body will be starved of the energy it needs, and that means you won't be able to function as you would like to.

Having great technical ability and well-developed skills is vital for anyone who wants to compete seriously in soccer.

But even if you possess great ability, you will still not be able to exploit your skills to their full potential if your body and muscles are not supplied with the right kind of fuel.

So, if you believe that playing soccer is simply about skill, then think again.

Proper nutrition is a must-have, not a choice, or at least not for serious players.

Monosaccharides

Monosaccharides (from the Greek words monos: single, sacchar: sugar) are the most basic units of carbohydrates.

They are the simplest form of sugar and are colorless, water-soluble, crystalline solids. The list below contains some examples of different kinds of monosaccharide:
- Glucose (dextrose)
- Fructose (laevulose)
- Lactose
- Xylose
- Ribose

Your body absorbs monosaccharides through the cell wall that lines your small intestine.

From here, they are transported into the bloodstream from where they get stored as energy.

When monosaccharides remain in the body for too long without being used for energy, they are then converted into fat and stored in the fat tissue.

Fructose is an example of this kind of monosaccharide.

The body treats fructose in a different way to other carbohydrates.

Carbohydrates typically pass through the liver, where the body decides whether to use them as energy immediately or store them as glycogen for later use.

Yet studies have shown that fructose bypasses the liver altogether and is instead directly metabolized by the body.

Any amount that is not required immediately is then stored as glycogen.

Monosaccharides provide your body with an excellent, balanced form of energy.

However, as with any food, they should be consumed only in moderation.

Disaccharides

Disaccharides (meaning 'two sugars') are found in nature as lactose, sucrose, and maltose.

They are carbohydrates that feature high-up on the glycemic index.

This means they are rapidly broken down and thus cause a sharp rise in blood glucose levels.

Sucrose, which is formed by glucose and fructose, is what is typically used as table sugar.

Lactose is a key component of milk (you may have heard of lactose-intolerance or milk allergy) and is formed by glucose and galactose.

Unlike lactose and glucose, maltose is not a natural substance, so it has to be manufactured from different elements of carbohydrate.

Polysaccharides

Polysaccharides are complex carbohydrates. Complex carbohydrates are made up of sugar molecules and can be found in foods such as, beans, whole grains, peas, and other vegetables.

Because of their size, Polysaccharides are easily converted into glucose energy (blood sugar) by the body.

Protein

Protein is crucial for growth and tissue repair. It also helps to maintain a strong immune system.

It is vital for making essential enzymes and hormones. Protein is found in its highest concentrations in red meat, nuts, fish, and milk.

Approximately 15% of your daily calorie intake should be formed by protein.

This will help your body to recover quicker after games and stay resilient against injuries.

You may have been ordered by your coach at some point to 'put some muscle on those bones' in order to develop a stronger performance on the field.

The only way to do this is by consuming enough protein. Protein is vital for any attempts you make to strengthen up.

It is the key ingredient (along with exercise) needed by your muscles to expand and become stronger.

Soccer players should eat around 0.6 to 0.8 grams of protein per pound of body weight, per day, as a way to repair muscle tissue, assist muscle growth, and maintain muscle strength.

Protein can also be utilized as a pre-match energy booster, although it won't provide you with same level of energy reserves as carbohydrates.

While there are many manufacturers of protein products, very few of them use the necessary ingredients/procedures to ensure the production of a high-quality protein that the body needs.

Indeed, some of the promotional spiel can, on some labels, of various products, be quite misleading.

To put it more bluntly, some companies offer products that are not what they claim to be, so this really is a case of buyer beware!

If you do plan to complement your protein intake with supplements, then you really need to be careful and research the market properly before buying into anything.

Make sure you only use a high quality product because it will be easier for your body to absorb and utilize the ingredients effectively.

A low quality protein product, on the other hand, could pass right through your system without adding any, or very little, benefit at all, thus making it nothing more than expensive urine.

There are also different types of protein products. So which of these are best suited for you and your needs?

Well, that depends on your specific requirements.

Below are some of the more common types of protein that you may want to check out.

Whey Protein

This is the most popular protein supplement on the market today.

Whey protein usually comes in powder form and is easy to dissolve in water.

This makes it simple to prepare, consume, and digest in the body.

Whey protein ranks high in biological value (BV), which is a measurement that is used to determine how well your body uses the nitrogen it processes from the protein.

Without going too technical, just know that nitrogen is a crucial nutrient that is used for muscle growth.

Some studies even claim that protein contains various components that can actually enhance the body's immune response.

Soy Protein

One reason why soy protein is not popular among soccer players is because it comes from a plant source.

This means it does not contain all of the essential amino acids that are required for muscle growth.

Also, many of the first soy products on the market were crude soy powders. These powders were full of sodium and carbohydrates.

However, this all-vegetable source of protein has gone through some big changes since it first hit the high streets.

Nowadays, soy protein contains complete protein, and also has one of the most efficient levels of digestibility of all protein sources.

Soy beans also contain very little fat and almost no cholesterol.

If you are lactose intolerant, you should at least consider soy protein as it is completely free of lactose.

Some studies have even ranked soy protein higher then beef, milk, and eggs; although in the wider scientific community, the jury is still out on that one.

Egg Protein

Eggs, regarded as an excellent source of protein, have featured heavily in fitness and protein-intensive diets since the early 1960s.

Dense quantities of protein are found in the eggs whites, and for this reason they are a great alternative to meat.

Egg protein is also highly-digestible, with about 97% of it being absorbed as amino acids, which can then be used by the body to synthesize new protein.

Fat

Fat is often associated with being fat or obese.

This has led the substance to take on negative connotations.

It is quite commonly assumed that all fat is bad for you, but it's not, as many professional soccer players, and other athletes, will tell you.

Fat is a source of essential fatty acids such as omega-3. They are called "essential" because the human body can't make them on its own.

Around 25% of your diet should consist of fat.

Fat is needed for growth and to and absorb vitamins and minerals.

However, not all fats are equal, and not all fats are good for your health either, so some types should be avoided. This is something that you really do need to be aware of.

Other types of fat, however, are good for you. In fact, some types of fat are essential for maintaining a healthy diet.

Yet it can often be overwhelming when trying to decipher which kinds of fat are good for you and those which are not.

Furthermore, some fats that are said to be healthy are recognizable by names like "Extra Virgin Olive Oil," for example, but even some of these might not be all that they seem.

This is because some brands, though not all brands, have other, unhealthy fats added to them, something which is not always obvious or even included in the small print.

To help guide you on the various fats out there I will describe the different kinds without using too much technical jargon.

OK, there are basically three different types of fat, namely saturated fats, unsaturated fats, and trans fats.

Saturated fats are those which are solid at room temperature.

Foods high in saturated fat come mainly from animals, though lesser amounts can be found in some plants.

Unsaturated fat comes with some health benefits and is the one fat that you should definitely consume.

Such fats are called polyunsaturated fatty acids and monounsaturated fats, and unlike saturated fats they remain in liquid form at room temperature.

The third type of fat is trans-fat or trans-fatty acid. Tran-fat is a bad fat and should be avoided at all costs.

This type of fat is uncommon in nature and formed artificially when oil goes through a process called hydrogenation, which basically means to treat with hydrogen.

Let's now look at each of these fats in a little more detail.

Saturated Fat

A high intake of saturated fat increases your cholesterol level and that in turn can contribute to high blood pressure, heart disease, and stroke.

Try not to include any more than 10% saturated fat into your diet at the most.

Any more than 10% and the harms outweigh the benefits.

Here are 10 products where you will typically find saturated fats:
1. Animal Fats
2. Butter
3. Cheese
4. Chocolate
5. Coconut
6. Cream (heavy, whipping)
7. Fish Oils
8. Hydrogenated Oils
9. Nuts & seeds
10. Processed Meats

On a side note, I would advise you to never eat any unhealthy snacks in front of your coach before a game or practice.

Believe me when I say, a coach may get very upset if he sees you disrespecting your body by chewing on any foods which are harmful to health.

He may even put you on the bench just to teach you a lesson. I have seen this happen on numerous occasions over the years.

Unsaturated Fats

Whenever possible, always choose unsaturated fats over saturated fats.

In contrast to saturated fats, this type of fat will actually lower your "bad" LDL cholesterol levels and also help you to burn off excess body weight.

Good sources of unsaturated fats in oils include:
- Olive oil
- Rapeseed oil
- Safflower oil (to name just three)

Polyunsaturated fat is a type of unsaturated fat that is especially beneficial to heart health.

Good sources of polyunsaturated fats include
- Butternuts
- Cashew nuts
- Herrings
- Mackerel
- Salmon
- Sardines
- Sunflower seeds
- Trout
- Tuna
- Walnuts

Monounsaturated fats are another type of unsaturated fat.

It is commonly found in plant-based foods, but can also be found in some meat and dairy products too.

Oils that contain monounsaturated fats are usually liquid when stored at room temperature, but they will start to turn solid when chilled below room temperature.

Good sources of monounsaturated fats include
- Butter
- Cheese (Parmesan cheese, Cheshire cheese, Cream cheese)
- Dark chocolate
- Eggs
- Fish
- Fruits (high fat) such as olives and avocados
- Nuts and seeds (various)
- Red meats
- Vegetable oils

My personal favorite source for unsaturated fats is cashew nuts.

They are incredibly moreish and I love to use them in my cooking.

The main disadvantage with these nuts is that I often eat too many (it's a weakness of mine).

This forces me to work harder during practice sessions so that I can burn off the extra calories.

If you like nuts and also find it hard to stop eating them once you start, then you should be prepared to work harder than the others in your team so that you avoid gaining unwanted pounds.

You have been warned!

Trans Fat

Trans fat is the most dangerous type of fat from a health perspective and by far the worst type of fat you can possibly consume.

This fat is uncommon in nature and is produced industrially from partially hydrogenated vegetable oil.

The human body doesn't really know how to process trans fats.

Trans-fats also increase the potential risk for developing heart disease, and also increases cholesterol levels (two other very good reasons to avoid them at all costs).

Trans fats are found in foods containing hydrogenated vegetable oils.

Here's a quick list of products to be wary of:
- Breakfast cereals
- Butter substitutes
- Deep-fried food (including most French fries)
- Doughnuts
- Packaged Foods
- Pastries, cakes
- Pizzas
- Processed creams
- Snack bars

Because the public has been made aware of the dangers of trans fats, food producers who use them in their products have been sneaky by hiding the term "trans fats" on the labelling.

They do this by showing alterative names, names less commonly known to the general public.

Typically, these alternative words are 'hydrogenated', or 'partially hydrogenated' but just know that these all mean one thing - trans fats.

The Micronutrients

Just like macronutrients (see chapter 1), micronutrients are also crucial for both good health and your performance on the field.

Micronutrients include various vitamins such as vitamins C, E, and K.

These vitamins are essential as they provide your body with the energy and nutrients it needs for you perform at your very best on the soccer field.

Vitamins and Soccer

Although regular practice, quality equipment, and the ability to play good soccer are all essential requirements for your overall development as a player, none of the above means very much if you are vitamin deficient.

Vitamins really do affect every aspect of your ability to play good soccer, from the quality of your eyesight to the speed of your crosses.

If you find that you're not developing as quickly as you would like to, then a lack of vitamins may be your problem.

You're probably wondering exactly what vitamins an up-and-coming soccer player should make sure are getting into his diet.

I will list some of the most important vitamins in this chapter.

These are the ones that you should definitely know about.

I will also be pointing out how these vitamins can enhance your game.

Most importantly, I will show you ways of getting more of them in your daily diet.

Vitamin A

Vitamin A is perhaps best known for its effect on eyesight.

Although it won't give you instant night vision, increasing your vitamin A intake will have a noticeable effect on your ability to see in low light situations.

Not having enough vitamin A, on the other hand, can cause problems with vision that may compromise your ability to play soccer at your full potential.

Vitamin A doesn't just affect vision though.

This multi-purpose vitamin also promotes healthy skin, bones, and teeth.

Fortunately, vitamin A can be found in a variety of foods, including eggs, meat, and dairy products, as well as in yellow, orange and green plants.

Vitamin A is a fat soluble vitamin, which means your body can store it until it is needed.

The B Vitamins

Have you ever wished you had just a little more bounce in your step?

Well, maybe the B vitamins can help.

Once thought to be a single vitamin, the B vitamins are now known to be a group of nutrients that are needed to convert oxygen and calories into energy, and for you that translates to more oomph on the field.

B Vitamins also help your body produce important things such as protein and blood cells.

Without them, your body simply would not be able to make new cells.

Furthermore, a deficiency in B vitamins may even put you at a higher risk of developing cancer and other chronic diseases.

If you become deficient in B vitamins, for whatever reason, you may find yourself missing games and practices due to illness.

That's because people who don't get enough B vitamins not only have less energy generally, but they are more prone to common illness than those who are not vitamin B deficient.

There are actually eight distinct B vitamins, but the good news is that they are often found in the same foods.

So providing you include these types of food into your daily diet, then there is no reason for you to become deficient in vitamin B.

If you're in need of that kick of energy that only B vitamins can give you, then you need to make sure you're getting enough of the following types of food onto your plate at mealtimes:
- Whole grains
- Seafood
- Meats
- Eggs
- Legumes
- Molasses
- Leafy green vegetables.

Many sports and energy drinks are also fortified with this energy-yielding group of vitamins.

Whether you're a carnivore or a vegetarian, it's not hard to find foods which containing vitamin B.

Point to note: Because the B vitamins are water soluble, it means your body cannot store them like it can fat soluble vitamins.

Because of this, you should include foods abundant in vitamin B into your "daily" diet.

Vitamin C

Are your injuries taking a little too long to heal, or are you fed up with catching every little bug that goes around?

If you answered yes to any of the above, then you are probably in need of some vitamin C.

It's hard to overstate the beneficial effects of this water soluble vitamin because it really is essential for assisting good health.

Vitamin C performs a variety of roles within your body, from stimulating the immune system to helping wounds heal quickly.

It can also help to fend off terminal diseases like cancer, by acting as an antioxidant.

People who don't receive an adequate amount of this essential vitamin can end up with the infamous scurvy disease; a disease which leads to tooth loss and a breakdown of the body's connective tissue.

Many people swear by the benefits of having a little vitamin C boost at the first signs of illness.

Some of the foods that are rich in vitamin C content also tend to be acidic.

Here is a shortlist of some foods containing vitamin C:
- Liver
- Broccoli
- Citrus fruits
- Tomatoes
- Berries
- Tropical fruits (most)

As you can see, adding vitamin C to your daily diet is not just a healthy choice, but a delicious one as well.

Vitamin D

If you want to have the strong bones needed for running and kicking, and bones that are resilient to rough tackles, then you need to make sure you're getting enough vitamin D in your diet.

This fat-soluble vitamin is important for both the development and the maintenance of strong healthy bones.

Vitamin D aids your ability to think clearly and also helps to lower high blood pressure.

Vitamin D can get into our system three ways.

It can be made in the skin from exposure to sunlight, it can be consumed through certain foods, and it can enter our body in the form of supplements, the latter usually being a last resort.

A good source of vitamin D can be had from the following foods:
- Beef liver
- Cheese

- Dairy products
- Egg yolks
- Fatty fish
- Fish oils
- Mushrooms
- Processed grains

Vitamin E

Most soccer players go through a lot of wear and tear during the course of a game.

This makes vitamin E particularly important because of its role in cell recovery.

It acts as an antioxidant, protecting cell membranes.

This fat-soluble vitamin also helps to form the red blood cells that are needed to carry oxygen around in the blood.

Without vitamin E in your system you won't be on the field for too long.

Vitamin E can be found in many types of food sources such as:
- Avocados
- Nuts
- Seeds
- Vegetable oils
- Whole grains

This is the one fat-soluble antioxidant that will make you healthier, faster, and fitter.

Vitamin K

Vitamin K is a very important vitamin as the body needs it for its blood-clotting function.

This makes it a crucial nutrient for soccer players, and indeed people everywhere, but especially in sports as that's where nasty cuts and bleeding are more likely to occur, more often.

Vitamin K is not only useful for its role in blood clotting.

It has other essential roles as well, like building strong bones and preventing heart disease to name just two, but there are some other important bodily processes that it plays a part in too.

Whichever way you look at it, this fat-soluble nutrient is important to your game, and so you need to keep vitamin K in your system by consuming the right foods.

There are several foods which are good sources of vitamin K, including:
- Dairy products
- Leafy green vegetables
- Meats
- Vegetable oils

All of the above foods, and a few others besides, provide enough vitamin K for you to recover from the cuts and scrapes that inevitably come about in the game of soccer.

OK, that concludes our brief look at the most important vitamins.

As you can see, taking vitamins by adding foods into your diet which include sufficient amounts of each can make a huge difference in your ability to play good soccer.

It's not difficult to get all the vitamins you need from foods, but it is important to know which foods contains what vitamins, and now you do.

Minerals

There is a lot of talk lately about minerals and the role they play in a healthy and active life.

But hearing about the importance of minerals from professional nutritionists doesn't tell us much more than they're important!

Such one-liners are obviously scant on details and this is why many people still have unanswered questions on the exact role minerals play in our bodies.

We want to know more!

As a soccer player, you should probably know something other than the fact that minerals are "good for you" so that you can use them to promote better health and fitness levels.

For this, you will need to know exactly what minerals do in your body, specifically, and most importantly, can they help you to become a better player than if you were say mineral deficient?

In other words, is this something worth the hassle of learning about?

In short, yes it is.

Knowing the 'mineral basics' is valuable information for you as a sports person.

OK, let's start to look at minerals in a little more detail.

What are minerals?

Minerals are also called micronutrients.

They are necessary organisms needed throughout our entire life, in small quantities.

Minerals primarily orchestrate a range of bodily functions that are essential for healthy living.

Because our bodies do not make these minerals naturally, we must therefore get them from our diet or from various supplements.

Although they make up less than four percent of the human body, many of our most crucial processes would not be able to function without essential minerals.

There are several minerals that all people need in their diet, namely:
- Potassium
- Sodium
- Calcium
- Phosphorus
- Magnesium
- Zinc
- Iron
- Iodine
- Manganese

Why do we need minerals - really?

Although there are many different minerals, most of them have a common denominator.

They are the building blocks of your body's cells; they are responsible for regulating different chemical reactions and processes.

Some minerals, such as calcium and manganese, help to build healthy bones.

Others, like iron, aid the body in producing healthy blood cells.

Each of the minerals plays a different yet essential role, all helping to build and maintain a strong and healthy you.

The healthier you are overall, the more capable you will become as a soccer player.

Having a well-nourished body at all times provides you with the requisite energy and strength needed to compete and participate as a valuable member of your team.

How do minerals affect soccer players?

It is imperative that all people, especially soccer players, get adequate amounts of all of the essential minerals, and then make sure they maintain those levels at all times.

Your body is being taxed to extremes whenever you participate in a competition or a tough training session.

You most likely leave every game not just with a heavy dose of fatigue, but also with a few bumps, bruises, and scrapes to boot.

It's crucial that you are able to restore your fatigued muscles as quickly as possible, but you also need to continue building on the stamina and strength you already have so that you can play even better next time.

Don't forget, until you reach your peak, there is always room for improvements.

Imagine not being able to heal quickly from a minor scrape, or even get up from a moderate fall because it's knocked the stuffing out of you.

This is what the reality looks like without an adequate amount of minerals in your system.

It's easy to see how getting enough minerals, or not getting enough minerals, can make all the difference to your game.

Making sure you have a healthy diet, one which includes all the necessary vitamins and minerals, prepares you for success on and off the field.

When a body is well-nourished and energized it makes you feel capable of doing anything, and that in turn has a positive impact on the way you feel mentally as well. In other words, it's all good.

Sodium and potassium

There are two mineral types that play a vital role in your body during your practice and games, namely sodium and potassium.

These two minerals are what's known as electrolytes, or salts in plain English.

They enter and exit your muscle cells during muscular contraction and relaxation.

Electrolytes reside in the blood, and other body fluids, and carry an electric charge.

They also affect the amount of water there is in your body at any given time, the acidity of your blood known as (pH), and your muscle function, along with a few other important processes.

When you are practicing or playing games, a large amount of these electrolytes are lost through your sweat.

When this happens, there is an imbalance in your body. You might have seen salt rings on your clothes after a game.

The lack of these salts can be harmful if they are not replenished.

You can often electrolytes advertised on the labels of various sports drinks (be sure to read the content label to make sure), so drinking these before, during and after your practice and games might be something you want to look into.

Electrolytes can also be found in some energy bars too.

However, if you prefer to skip sugary sports drinks then nutrient-rich fruits, vegetables, dairy, and whole grains are the natural way to stock up on, and replace minerals lost during vigorous activity.

In fact, many professional players might prefer to consume a salty soup or other foods containing electrolytes as their pre-game meal.

Calcium

So, why do you need calcium?

Well, you probably remember your parents telling you as a little kid that you should drink lots of milk because it's good for your teeth, nails and bones, and that it will help you to grow stronger. They were not wrong.

Milk is a definitely great source of calcium along with yogurt, and cheese too, but some types are better than others.

Dairy is certainly the best know source of calcium but isn't the only food type to contain this important nutrient (see list below).

To improve your calcium intake and have your opponents bouncing off your strong body during a game, be sure to include some or all of the following foods into you regular diet:

- Low Fat Cheese
- Low Fat Yogurts
- Non Fat or 1% Milk
- Non-daily foods include:
- Cereals
- Fruits (various)
- Leafy greens
- Legumes
- Seafood

Numerous foods and drinks are also fortified with the mineral, but always opt for the more natural sources whenever possible.

Remember this: if you're not getting enough calcium in your diet, then your body will take what it needs from your bones.

It has to do this to ensure normal cell function.

But the problem with taking calcium from your bones on a regular basis is that it can lead to weakened bones, and you certainly don't want that to happen.

So make sure you get all the calcium your body needs by including calcium-rich foods into your regular diet.

Iron

Iron works as a transporter of oxygen throughout your body.

If you don't get enough of it during practice and games, the effects are immediate.

If your iron levels are low then you'll get tired pretty quickly.

In other words, your performance on the field will deteriorate drastically.

To prevent iron deficiency from happening you will need to include iron-rich foods into your regular meals.

Don't worry, those of you who already eat balanced meals will already be doing this, meaning you won't need to adjust your diet very much, if at all (see list below).

The most common iron-rich foods include the following:
- Brown rice
- Dark-green leafy vegetables
- Dried fruits
- Eggs

- Fish
- Iron-fortified cereals or bread
- Nuts and seeds
- Pulses and beans
- Tofu
- White and red meats

Some people, for various reasons, can't get enough iron into their bloodstream, or the iron they do have is not being processed as it should be.

Deficiency of iron is a common cause of anemia or more specifically, iron-deficiency anemia.

Typical symptoms include:
- Tiredness and lethargy
- Shortness of breath
- Heart palpitations (noticeable heartbeats)
- Pale complexion

As you can see, three of the four symptoms above will mean you'll not be much use to yourself or anyone else on the soccer field.

You will also be feeling downright miserable as well, until you can get yourself back together.

If, for whatever reason you become iron deficient, then the missing iron can be restored and delivered by the taking of supplements (something a lot of people do).

However, it's always best to get a proper diagnosis from a physician so that he can prescribe you with the correct supplement at the right dosage.

Perhaps the most commonly prescribed supplement is one called Ferrous Sulphate, which is taken in tablet form two to three times daily.

Again, even if you recognize the symptoms above, NEVER try to self-diagnose, and NEVER self-prescribe for iron-deficiency or any other health condition.

Zinc

Zinc is sometimes referred to as the building block of your body.

It helps the body to repair and grow tissues, which is obviously very important, especially after you become injured and need your body to react fast in the healing process.

Zinc is what's known as an essential trace element, which is a fancy way of saying we have to have it in order to survive.

To get adequate amounts of zinc into your system, you'll need to consume the following foods:
- Breads
- Cereal products
- Dairy foods
- Meats
- Shellfish

Remember, zinc is vital for many of the body's biological functions, so make sure you get enough of it into your diet by consuming some or all of the food types above.

Diets

Ask any professional soccer player and he will surly tell you of the importance of eating right.

Consuming a carefully-attuned diet, along with drinking plenty of fluids, is fundamental to any soccer player's performance on the field.

The Atkins Diet?

If you are a soccer player you should try to avoid the Atkins diet and other Atkins-type diets at all costs.

This is because the Atkins diet requires that you eat plenty of protein while avoiding most carbohydrates.

Without a good intake of quality carbohydrates, you'll not be able to perform at peak-levels on the field.

This is because carbohydrates provide your main source of fuel when practicing or playing soccer.

Before each training session and game you should already be stocked-up on good-quality carbs.

This will ensure that you can play at your full potential as the carbs provide you with the energy you need.

When you have good energy levels you can play with power, skill, and maintain your stamina for the duration of the game.

The almost carb-free Atkins diet and other low-carb eating plans, can significantly and detrimentally affect your performance.

A solid soccer diet should consist of at least 45% carbohydrates, with 25% proteins and 30% fat.

Any major variation to the above will see a drop in your performance.

It really is as simple as that.

This means you need to make carbohydrates your main food source, and indeed the foundation of your diet.

Quality, staple carbs include pasta, rice, and potatoes.

However, it's not just about the carbs.

The most important thing here is balance, so you mustn't dismiss the importance of proteins and fats in the diet either.

You just need to regulate how much you consume of each.

Protein is essential for a balanced diet.

It not only helps to build strong bones and muscles, but it also aids in the body-repair process after strenuous games and injuries.

Fat is also essential for general health and wellbeing.

It strengthens your immune system and helps protect against illness.

Good fats can be found in oily and fatty fish.

These are a rich source of omega-3 fatty acids, which is a type of fat that is extremely good for health.

It would be futile trying to play regular soccer on an Atkins-style diet. Sooner, rather than later, you would find yourself having to switch back to a more traditional diet.

In brief, the absence of carbohydrates in your meals would have a very negative impact on your ability to play at your best.

I am not saying that the Atkins diet, or any other low-carb style diet, is bad in general.

In fact, it is very useful for people who need to lose weight fast for health reasons, and perhaps for others who don't participate in fast, physical sporting activities.

However, the Atkins diet is not a soccer diet because it will not provide you with the necessary fuel to practice, play, and recover.

Organic Diet

Organic diets are an excellent way to build and maintain good health and fitness.

Before I describe how an organic diet can do this, I will first explain precisely what an organic diet actually is.

Many think of the word 'organic' to mean raw-foods. This is not the case, however.

The term organic refers to food that has been grown using conventional farming methods, that is, without the use of harmful chemical agents.

In other words, a return to basic farming procedures; practices that were in place long before all these pesticides, fungicides and herbicides became the norm; many of which are said to poison the earth.

The consequence of consuming non-organic foods means there is always a potential threat to human health whenever we eat items grown using modern agricultural methods.

This is because the chemicals from the agents that are used on crops are then ingested into the body. That can't be good for human health, it just can't be.

The result of intensive, modern-day farming has also meant that the soil has gradually become depleted of its natural nutrients.

Nutrient-depleted soil means that the crops grown in it are also lacking in nutritional value compared to crops grown in soil which is not nutrient deficient, as is the case with an organic farm.

So raw food does not necessarily mean it is organic food.

You can have raw-organic or raw non-organic food.

Raw simply means food which is not cooked or processed.

Eating raw, organic foods is an excellent way of providing your body with the right kinds of nutrients, and without ingesting harmful toxins in the process.

Raw food, in general, contains many more naturally-occurring vitamins and minerals than food which is cooked or processed, and especially raw-organic food.

These essential vitamins and minerals are what help the body to function smoothly and gain resilience against disease and injury.

And in the case where we do become sick or injured, the healthier our diet has been, the sooner we are likely to recover from any ailment.

Anyone looking to obtain maximum health and fitness will combine an organic diet with a regular intake of fluids so that they remain in a hydrated state at all times.

Water is the best fluid you can drink, without exception, and best of all is that fresh drinking water it's easily and freely available, in most western countries, so make good use of your tap.

Under normal circumstances, you ought to aim for at least 10 large (33cl) glasses of water each day to maintain your hydration levels.

Most people don't, by the way, much to their detriment.

Whenever folks start to tire later in the day, it's often because they are experiencing the early stages of dehydration, and not because they're exhausted by their work or some physical activity.

Water also assists your body in flushing out toxins.

Some of the raw food types you can include into your diet (cucumber and watermelon as two examples) will also count as part of your overall fluid intake.

Keeping to an organic diet, combined with the consumption of plenty of fresh-water, will provide your body with all that it needs to perform at its optimal levels. It's a simple recipe for success.

Soccer Diet Example

A healthy diet filled with quality energy-rich foods will enable your performance-levels to increase exponentially.

Eating unhealthy foods, on the other hand, will have the opposite effect.

A suitable diet for soccer players should be carb-rich. What foods and how much exactly will be adjusted slightly whenever a game and practice session is nearing.

Avoid unhealthy processed foods, fast foods, and snack foods such as hamburgers or candy.

As tasty and as tempting as these might be to you, just know that they play no role in the life of an up-and-coming, or already successful, soccer player, especially before a game.

The following table contains a balanced dietary plan that is suitable for any soccer player:

Breakfast	**Lunch**	**Dinner**
Milk (of a low-fat variety)	Fish (rich in Omega 3 fatty acid)	Chicken (skinless)
Pancakes	Pasta	Lean meat
Potatoes	Bread (wholemeal). Multigrain bread is far superior to white bread)	Rice (brown or white)
Fruits	Soups	Vegetables
Yoghurt	Salad (without dressing)	

Fluid

In this chapter you are about to discover the true importance of fluids, or more specifically, hydration.

This is something which can literally make or break your game.

Hydration

A game of soccer exerts extreme demands on the body.

One of the key ways of combatting the effects of these demands is to remain properly hydrated at all times.

This involves the regular consumption of clean, healthy liquids, preferably water, to replace the fluids you lose through perspiration during the game.

Indeed, as your body heats up, it starts to sweat profusely in its attempt to try and cool you down.

Just like a car engine requires water to prevent it from overheating, so too does the human body.

It is not only during matches that you'll need to remember to stay hydrated.

Any practice games, training sessions, and periods of exercise must all be carried out while being sufficiently hydrated.

In a nutshell, if you're not properly hydrated then you won't be able to perform at your best and nor will you feel in peak condition.

Hydration tips:
- Always quench your thirst. In fact, you shouldn't even wait until you're thirsty before you drink.
- Milk can be drunk on occasion as a water replacement. Aim for the skimmed or semi-skimmed variety.
- The occasional sports drink can also count as a water replacement, although be cautious of these. Most sports drinks are loaded with excess sugar and should be consumed in moderation or after strenuous bouts of physical activity. If you maintain good, regular hydration levels, then there should be no need to consume sports drinks to replenish loss fluids under normal circumstances.

- Avoid all sodas and any carbonated beverages that contain tons of sugar, additives, and preservatives.
- Drinks containing caffeine (tea, coffee, and cola) make you pee more frequently and therefore counteract the hydration process. Drink such beverages in moderation and avoid them altogether on game days.

Dehydration

Dehydration is the term used to describe the state that your body enters when you do not have the appropriate amounts of fluid in your system.

You are losing valuable fluids all the time, when you sweat, urinate, vomit, have diarrhea, and even when you breathe.

If you do not regularly replace the lost water from your body, then you will soon begin to suffer the effects of early dehydration.

For soccer players, dehydration is a particularly common problem during games, especially those which are played under a hot sun, where profuse sweating and heavy breathing causes significant water loss in a relatively short space of time.

I know from experience that many amateur players simply don't take on board enough water during games; something that serves to their disadvantage.

Here are the five primary symptoms of early dehydration:

1. Feeling very thirsty

2. Feeling lightheaded
3. A quickened heartbeat
4. Dryness around the mouth and lips
5. Infrequent urination and/or dark colored and strong-smelling urine

Water

Water is highly undervalued as a component of a good soccer diet among amateurs.

Most professional players prefer to drink water rather than sugary sports drinks, not because they favor the taste of water, which is pretty flavorless anyway, but because they know that it is by far the best fluid for keeping the body in a hydrated state.

Sports or caffeine-based drinks provide a good energy boost but will not replenish your fluids in the same way that water will.

They may even contribute to dehydration when drunk in large quantities.

Providing you maintain a regular regime whereby you never allow yourself to become dehydrated, then water is your best choice of fluid.

Not only will your body stay hydrated, but you will you also feel fitter and stronger and therefore get to boost your performance on the field because of this.

Another thing worth mentioning is that dehydrated muscles are much more likely to cramp-up and fatigue quicker than muscles that are hydrated and functioning normally.

The best hydration advice is for you to never allow yourself to get thirsty in the first place.

If you feel thirsty during a game or a practice session, especially soon after the start, then it is most likely too late to do much about it.

Even if you down a bucketful of water, it's not going to help much.

If anything, it will probably hinder you further because of the large volume of water that now lies heavily in your stomach.

Preempt your thirst by drinking small amounts at regular intervals.

This is the best way to permanently stave off dehydration and to prevent the above scenario ever happening to you.

It is advisable to keep a sports bottle full of water with you at all times.

This way, you can maintain your hydration without needing to look for a tap or a store that sells bottled water whenever you're out and about.

I've actually made this into a healthy habit.

What that means is if I do happen to leave the house without my water, I never get more than a few steps away before I notice it's missing.

I actually like to freeze my water overnight because this way it's kept nice and refreshingly cold during the day.

As mentioned earlier in the chapter, an excellent way of telling whether your body is becoming dehydrated or not is by the color of your urine.

So next time you go to the bathroom remember to check the color of your pee.

Healthy urine contains substances which give it its light yellow tint.

If your urine is dark orange it means these substances are undiluted, and that indicates that you are now in the early stages of dehydration.

The darker it is, the more you will need to drink in order to replenish lost fluids.

How much is enough?

There is an unofficial standard when talking about the amount of water you should consume each day.

In fact, there is much confusion in the scientific community about hydration and just how much fluid we should drink on average, under various conditions.

Let's not forget too, that some people perspire a lot more than others, and obviously they become dehydrated quicker as a consequence.

The unofficial standard recommends that we drink at least 8-10 full glasses (33cl) of water per day, under normal conditions.

However, when you are participating in soccer training or games, this standard obviously goes out of the window because these conditions are far from normal.

The more you exert yourself, the more water you will need to consume to replenish those lost fluids, and as you know, there's plenty of physical exertion happening on a soccer field.

The minimum amount of water you should probably drink during a 24 hour period should be no less than three liters.

You will need to drink plenty of water before a game so that you're nicely hydrated at kickoff.

It's important to drink water during the game as well because you need to maintain your hydration levels.

You also need to continue drinking water at regular intervals after the final whistle has blown.

It is recommended that you drink 1-2 liters about two hours before your game.

Whether it's one or two liters depends on your hydration level before the two hours prior to kickoff.

During the game, you should try to consume about 7-10 ounces every fifteen to twenty minutes whenever possible.

Improved performance

You will not improve your ball skills just by drinking water per se.

However, your overall performance on the field will be much better than if you were to play in a more dehydrated state. That is a certainty.

Improved performance means both physically and mentally.

You will, for example, be able to run and work harder for longer periods without tiring.

Furthermore, your concentration will also be higher, which makes you more alert generally, thus minimizing the potential for mistakes.

Not enough water

If your body is short on water then you'll start to dehydrate pretty quickly.

That means you may begin to feel weak and dizzy as a consequence, especially if you keep pushing yourself hard while in this state.

If you do begin to feel less than normal, then you really should take immediate action.

Ignoring the symptoms could result in you actually fainting or collapsing; something that is not all that uncommon among amateur players.

The amount of water you consume before, during, and after a game depends largely on the weather.

During hot summer days you will obviously need to consume more water than you would do when playing in cold weather.

Sports Drinks

We've already touched lightly on the topic of sports drinks and now we're going to look at them a little more closely.

Today, we are constantly bombarded with ads on the television on the internet and in print, all of which urge us to consume their sweet and colorful sports drinks, convincing us, or trying to convince us, that these all-refreshing, all-hydrating beverages are the best invention since sliced bread.

But are they, really?

Quite often, a trusted celebrity is the face of the product, suggesting that you too can feel or achieve what they feel or achieve as a direct result of consuming whatever sports drink it is they're promoting.

So what are these miracle products?

What exactly makes a drink a sports drink?

Who needs them?

And do they really make a difference?

OK, let's look at each of these questions in turn.

What is a sports drink?

A sports drink is intended to help athletes, and other active people, recover quickly from extreme levels of activity.

They offer more than your average beverage because they do more than just replenish lost fluids.

As well as including salts and sugars, which help to quickly hydrate a dehydrated body, sports drinks also include various nutrients.

These nutrients help to restore the body's electrolyte balance.

The liquid carbohydrates contained within these beverages give a much needed energy boost to an otherwise tired athlete.

Sports drinks are not only healthier than many other types of beverages sold in high-street refrigerators, but they are also tastier too, and therefore more palatable than plain water.

The health factor, combined with nice flavors, has made sports drinks a favorite among athletes from every sport.

But are they really needed?

The answer to that is no, not really, not if you can maintain your hydration levels with pure water consumption, which is generally the best option.

And sports drinks should definitely not replace your daily water intake.

Do soccer players need sports drinks?

In some cases, sports drinks can be very helpful to soccer players, particularly when playing hard in a high-tempo game for an extended period of time under a hot summer sun.

In situations like this you'll be sweating excessively, losing not just fluids, but also electrolytes.

So sometimes it's better for soccer players to get a little energy boost from sports drinks, especially when playing under conditions like the one mentioned above.

Replacing fluid without addressing the loss of minerals can result in a dangerous condition known as water intoxication.

Drinking a sports drink replaces not just the fluids lost, but the electrolytes as well.

Despite the obvious advantages of consuming sports drinks, there is, nevertheless, a balance that needs to be struck here.

So the secret is getting to know your own body well, and understand how to best to maintain its hydration levels.

This way, you will become more involved in prevention than you will be cure, which is a much better way to be.

Making your own sports drinks

Sports drinks bought in plastic bottles can be both expensive and bad for the environment.

For this reason, many amateur soccer players simply drink water instead.

However, drinking only water can, on occasions, result in an electrolyte imbalance, especially if the body is not maintained properly by good diet.

Anyone who does have an electrolyte imbalance, even a mild one, can't expect to perform as well as they would do if they didn't have this imbalance.

There is an alternative to the costly and fancy-packaged sports drinks sold in high street stores, and it comes in the form of a powder.

These powdered options are simply added to water then stirred.

That's it.

You now have a cheaper, yet still just as good, homemade sports drink made from a basic formula.

If you would like to have a little more control in making your own sports drinks from powders, then there are several commercially available brands that are popular among soccer players.

These powders come in a wide range of flavors so it should be easy enough to find something you enjoy.

Note that these powdered drinks will all vary somewhat according to their carbohydrate (CHO) and electrolyte content, along with the addition of other ingredients.

This is obviously a less expensive option than the bottled varieties.

However, if you really want to keep the costs right down and have full control over both the contents and the flavor, then why not make your own sports drinks from scratch?

This is an incredibly simple process where all you need are a few basic ingredients from around the kitchen, namely fruit squash or juice, sugar, salt, and water.

With a bit of imagination you now have a low-cost sports drink that meets all your rehydration needs, and also one that tastes exactly how you want it to taste.

So as you can see, getting the electrolytes you need to replenish lost body fluids doesn't need to be expensive, difficult, or bad for the planet.

A quick search online will reveal a plethora of homemade recipes for you to try at your leisure.

Alternative Hydration

During a competitive soccer game, energy and water is drained from the body at an alarming rate. While there is no magic drink to give you your energy back in nanoseconds, you can still take concrete steps to rehydrate yourself in the fastest way possible.

While water and sports drinks are generally considered the best choices for hydration, there are several other options that can contribute toward giving your body the water it needs.

These supplementary options are various food items.

They not only contribute to your water intake, but they also give you some welcome variety from drinking only liquids:

- **Watermelon**: Not only is this fruit 92 percent water, but it also offers a wide range of nutrients and vitamins too, all of which help you to stay in peak form. The best way to bring watermelon to the field is to throw some cold watermelon cubes in a thermos or cooler where they can be kept nice and chilled.
- **Grapes**: These also have a high percentage of water content and contain some very key nutrients. They are also a neat, portable, mess-free snack that can either be kept cool in a cooler or eaten at room temperature.

- **Jell-O**: Most people know that gelatin is almost entirely water, but few think of it in terms of a rehydration option. You can store a gelatin mix in a thermos or a cooler, just like watermelon. To hydrate powdered gelatin, simply sprinkle it in cold water and let it sit for 5-10 minutes before drinking (it takes at least that long to dissolve in cool water). Just be sure to keep it cool, or it may turn into gelatin water, which is not something you will want to consume as that's a kind of sticky liquid.
- **Cucumbers**: Cucumbers are yet another natural food which is a good source of water. In fact, a cucumber is around 90 percent water. Not only are the cucumber peels rich in insoluble fiber, which helps to maintain a healthy digestive system, but these nourishing snacks also contain vitamin A and vitamin C. Try to keep your cucumbers cool because they are a crunchier, more refreshing snack when chilled.

Below are a few bad hydration alternatives in drink form, along with the reasons why they are not very good choices.

Despite this fact, some folks still opt for them as their hydration solution, although they probably wouldn't do for much longer if they read this list.

- **Caffeinated beverages**: Caffeine naturally dehydrates because of its diuretic effect (makes you pee more often). Therefore, even though caffeine drinks are still fluids, they contribute toward dehydration, not hydration.

- **High sugar juices**: Fructose, the sugar naturally present in fruits, actually slows down the process that the body goes through when absorbing water. Drinking it can actually make you feel sick because the fluid will slosh around uncomfortably as it waits to be absorbed.
- **Carbonated drinks**: These can cause bloating and make you too uncomfortable to play at your full potential. Further, almost all of these drinks include phosphoric acid in the ingredients, something which reduces calcium in the bones.

The secret to staying hydrated is to increase your intake of hydrating foods and beverages while decreasing your intake of anything that has a dehydrating effect in the body.

By sticking to this simple rule you should be able to maintain your hydration without too much fuss.

Now that you know of the several different foods and drinks that help with hydration, you can now enjoy a variety of options that will help you to be consistent in hydrating yourself at all times.

Game Food

No this is not a side chapter on wild animals and birds (game) that are hunted and eaten, but a chapter on soccer nutrition.

Here I will explain the best types of food to consume before, during and after a game.

We will also look at what you should eat when playing games in the morning or late evening.

The morning game

I don't know about you, but personally I used to hate early morning games.

The reason for this was that I always felt a lack of energy at that time of day.

Heck, I couldn't even participate in the warmup without wanting to rest halfway through.

However, this was all before I discovered the secret behind eating the right kinds of food.

These are meals that prepare you specifically for early morning activity.

The foods in the table below will charge your body with plenty of much needed energy.

Once you start to consume foods from this list you will be able to perform in the early morning without having to drag your feet every step of the way.

The days of getting tired just 10 minutes after the starting whistle is blown will become a thing of the past.

There will be no more hoping it all ends soon just so that you can crawl back home and take a good long nap.

For this change to happen, you are going to need to know how to consume the right kind of fuel.

These foods will give you the power you need for performing at your best in those early morning games of soccer.

Below is a table listing the early morning superfoods, including items to avoid (shown in the last column).

Meal	**Drinks**	**Dessert**	**Avoid**
Bagels	Apple Juice	Fruit Bar	Bacon
Oatmeal	Orange Juice	Fruit	Sausage
Bread	Vegetable Juice	Raisins	Butter
Yogurt	Hot chocolate	Banana	All Fried foods.

Evening game

Like many soccer players, I prefer to play games in the evening.

This is because I always feel more prepared at that time of day.

It is also easier to organize meals because I don't need to stress about time when preparing and cooking food later in the day.

In the table below I have listed some examples of the foods that I consume in preparation for evening games, including items to avoid (shown in the last column).

The variation and combination of meals that can be had from this list is limited only by your imagination.

Meal	Drinks	Dessert	Avoid
Spaghetti	Orange Juice	Cheese	Sugar
Chicken & Salad	Vegetable Juice	Popcorn	Chocolate
Salad	Water	Fruit	Chips
Fish & Potatoes	Fruit Juice	Pretzels	Tacos

Post-Game

The main purpose for consuming foods and beverage directly after a practice session or game is to rehydrate your body and replenish your muscles with new energy.

The table below gives you suggestions on what to eat post-match in order to get the most benefit, and also includes items to avoid (shown in the last column).

My favorite combination is to eat a fruit salad, drink plenty of water (although not in one go), and finish off with a tasty energy bar.

Sometimes it can be quite hard to eat anything just 30-60 minutes after a game is over.

The reason for this is because the hard physical exertion expended in a lively game of soccer can, in some people, suppress appetite.

If you have that "I'm just not hungry" feeling, then try to at least eat a protein bar, a couple of bananas, or a small sandwich made with white bread.

Here's the table of suggested food items best consumed directly after a game or practice session.

Meal	Drinks	Dessert	Avoid
Honey	Energy Drinks	Fruit Bars	Bacon
Bagel	Water	Fruit	Sausage
Banana	Lemonade	Raisins	Butter
Jams	Vegetable Juice	Bars	Fried Foods

Myths, Tips and Maximum Performance

There are a lot of false truths circulating about soccer diets nowadays. These can be very confusing to a lot of people, especially when you are new to the world of nutrition.

There will always be a few people who have never even glanced at a soccer nutrition book yet feel qualified to give advice on what should and should not be eaten as part of a soccer player's diet.

This is information that's quite often picked up and passed on by others who are equally unauthorized on the topic and therefore sets a bad precedent.

Common myths

To help you navigate this minefield of information, and more importantly the misinformation that's out there, I will debunk some of the more common myths related to soccer nutrition, and look at how various foods affect performance on the field.

Your performance is not affected by what you eat

This is complete and utter nonsense and one myth that you should disregard totally.

Your performance is very much influenced by what you eat.

The better the nutritional quality of the food you consume, the better your performances will be.

It really is as simple as that.

You just can't gorge on a slice of fudge cake a few hours before a game and expect to be on top form.

It may be hard to resist, but you must stay away from this type of unhealthy snacking, at least on game days, particularly if you're serious about developing as a player.

What you eat after a game doesn't affect your recovery

Every amateur soccer player has feasted on some of the worst possible post-match foods ever, namely chips, sodas, and chocolate bars.

This kind of junk scoffing should be avoided at all costs. Intelligent post-match eating will include fruits, energy bars, and plenty of water (see table above for a list of recommended post-game food items).

A sufficient quantity of good-quality carbohydrates is required after a match to help your body recover properly.

Sugary, salty, processed snacks just can't do that for you.

It doesn't matter if you eat one, two or five hours before a game

Oh yes it does.

You should make sure you leave at least four hours between eating and kick-off time.

In some circumstances, like early morning games for example, you may reduce this time to three hours, but certainly no less than that.

Your body ideally needs at least four hours to digest and process the foods you consume.

One of the most energy-efficient pre-match meals is spaghetti and meat sauce.

The combination of the sauce and the pasta gives you a meal that is both carb and protein-rich.

A simple meal like this will give you a significant energy boost that will enable you to last the duration of a game without feeling fatigued half way through.

Drinking or not drinking water doesn't affect your performance

Anyone who buys into this myth should try and play while they're not properly hydrated and seen how they fare.

Of course, consuming adequate amounts of water is essential to your success on the field.

Not only should you drink small amounts of water at set intervals before a game, but also while the game is going on, and after it has finished.

In other words, hydration is an ongoing practice (see chapter four for details).

A soccer club should keep plenty of accessible water on the sidelines and behind the goals so that players can stock-up on water reserves quickly and easily during games.

Remember, your body is like a car in as much as without fuel, or the wrong type of fuel, it will either not work or not perform as well as it should do.

Proper food and clean drinking water is premium fuel for the human body.

So make sure you keep your water intake high by getting into the habit of drinking at least two liters of the stuff in the hours leading up to a game or practice session.

Maximize your performance levels

Performing at your peak on the field means more than just putting in 100% effort while you are there. Being committed is crucial, but it is only one part of your overall soccer success.

You must also pay close attention to the finer details of your preparation off the field as well as giving your full focus while on it.

Indeed, soccer development is like a small puzzle, meaning there are various pieces to it that all need to be put into place, in the right order, before everything finally comes together.

If you have just one piece left out of the puzzle, or put in the wrong place, the outcome will be detrimental to your performance levels.

OK, let us now look at these simple, yet essential pieces of the "soccer success puzzle" in more detail.
- Rest
- Nutrition
- Sleep
- Focus

Sufficient rest

Before every game or training session you need to ensure you have had enough rest so that your body is fully energized and prepared for the rigors ahead.

Therefore, it's important that you don't get involved in any other form of physical activity for 24 hours before kick-off.

As you rest you can pursue anything that helps you to relax.

That might be kicking back to watch TV, playing video games, listening to music, reading a book, or whatever else works for you.

It really doesn't matter what it is as long as it doesn't require physical exertion.

Quality Nutrition

The importance quality nutrition cannot be overstated.

Consuming the proper kinds of food is vital to your soccer development and overall performance.

Without adequate nutrition, neither your body nor your mind will be able to function at its optimum.

In other words, your performance will be inhibited to some degree, depending on how undernourished you are at the time.

Again, we can use the car analogy to think about this.

If I fill my car with lots of premium fuel, it will go a long way, but if I only put a small amount in, and a substandard fuel at that, then it will need refilling again soon afterward plus it will perform poorly when it is running.

Your body is no different.

Fill it with low quality food and drink (fuel) and you will not only soon run out of energy, but your performance will be below par too.

The main type of fuel needed by your body for playing successful soccer is carbohydrates.

This energy source can be found in foods like pasta, bread, potatoes, rice, and various fruits.

It's important to remember, however, that not all carbohydrates are a good source of fuel for soccer players.

These are the "simple carbohydrates" and found mainly in processed foods like chips, candy, and soda drinks.

None of these things will bring you any lasting, positive energy as they contain what is known as empty calories, that is, calories derived from foods which contain no nutritional value.

Enough Sleep

Ever participated in a game after a poor night's sleep? If you haven't, I can tell you from experience that it is not a nice occurrence at all, in fact it can be torture.

To put it simply, without at least eight hours of quality kip (the average required by most of us), then your body will not be sufficiently rested for it to achieve peak performance, or certainly not from the start to the end of a game.

If you are having trouble sleeping, don't stress about it and try not to force yourself as this will only make things a whole lot worse.

The best approach for dealing with sleeplessness is not to think but to act.

So instead of endlessly tossing and turning and clock-watching, get out of bed and do something like reading or watching TV.

Stay up until you feel tired enough to return to bed. The reason for getting up and reading or watching television is to direct your mind away from whatever it is that's keeping you awake.

Under no circumstances should you start thinking or fretting about the next day's game, if that's what's keeping your mind active.

Change your focus and your focus will change.

Focus

Focusing while actively playing soccer can be easier said than done as many will testify.

It is very important, however, that you learn how to fully concentrate on the game you are participating in.

Don't let your mind wander or become distracted by something or someone else.

If you do, you've just become less valuable on the field.

One example of how focus can be disrupted is if your coach tells you to play out of position.

Even if you don't like the idea, you must still put any negative thoughts out of your head and simply concentrate on the role you have been given.

Okay, so you may not like it, but it is still your job, and in cases like this you just have to think more about the broader team effort than your own dissatisfaction.

Other things that can affect your focus include the equipment you are using, the weather, the condition of the pitch, personal problems, screaming spectators, pretty girls in the crowd, and so on and so forth.

Many amateur soccer players tend not to value the importance of focus too much.

Indeed, they may not even be aware that they easily lose concentration during a game. Yet all of the aforementioned items are fundamental for playing great soccer.

I would challenge anyone to play a game after a sleepless night, or without proper nutrition, and with a lack of focus, and see how they fare. Their performance, or lack or, would say it all.

On the flip side, playing soccer with all the aforementioned under control, nutrition, rest, and focus, and the achievement level will be totally opposite to that of players who fall short in these areas.

Nutrition checklist

To help you with your soccer nutrition I have composed a 12 point soccer nutrition checklist.

You might want to print this out and put it somewhere where it can't be avoided like on the refrigerator or you bedroom door, as two examples.

The 12 point Soccer Nutrition checklist:
1. Aim to eat a balanced and quality soccer diet each day.
2. Don't skip meals. Energy intake is crucial for your soccer performance and should not be neglected.
3. Aim to involve yourself in some form physical activity each day, outside of practice and games.
4. Ensure you sleep well as this will give your body time to repair itself and convert food into energy. Aim for between 7.5 to 8.5 hours a night. Don't sleep for more than 8.5 hours or any less than 7.5 hours if you are considered an "average sleeper".
5. Fast food is not an efficient source of energy or nutrition. Furthermore, over-consuming fast and processed foods will cause you to gain weight. The obvious consequence of weight gain will be that you become slower and less responsive on the field. Get into the habit of limiting your intake of these types of food to once a week or less.

6. Healthy snacks include foods which contain quality fats such as nuts, and fresh fruits which provide you with an excellent nutritional boost.
7. Calcium is essential for strong bones. Low-fat calcium sources like milk, cheese, and yogurt are good choices.
8. Iron, which helps deliver oxygen around the body, is a vital ingredient for soccer health and fitness. Fill up on iron by eating red meat and chicken.
9. A soccer diet also needs to contain zinc as this helps in growth and repair. It is vital for protecting against some injuries too, and for healing existing injuries.
10. Water should be your staple drink. Nothing quenches your thirst better.
11. When selecting foods to snack on, generally opt for those with little to no fat, salt, and sugar content.
12. A selection of fresh fruit is the healthiest and most nutritional snack you can have.

Becoming the best player that you can possibly be is all about dedication, patience, and relentless persistence.

Follow the suggested nutritional guidelines in this book and you have a great foundation on which to build your very own soccer success story.

End.

Ending...

My final piece of advice to you is this: If you have dreams do not give up on them, not even if someone you look up to says you can't do a thing. Remember to always, always, always believe in yourself, especially when stuff doesn't seem to be going according to plan, in fact, especially when stuff doesn't seem to be going according to plan.

Remember too, there cannot be any progress without some failure and setbacks along the way, there just can't be, and so be mindful of this whenever things get tough. If you don't believe in yourself then those who you need for encouragement and support won't be able to believe in you either. Be mindful of the fact that there is only one real failure in this life of ours and that is the failure to try. I sincerely wish you the very best in all your endeavors to succeed.

Mirsad Hasic

Made in the USA
Lexington, KY
31 October 2015